Who Lives on a Farm?

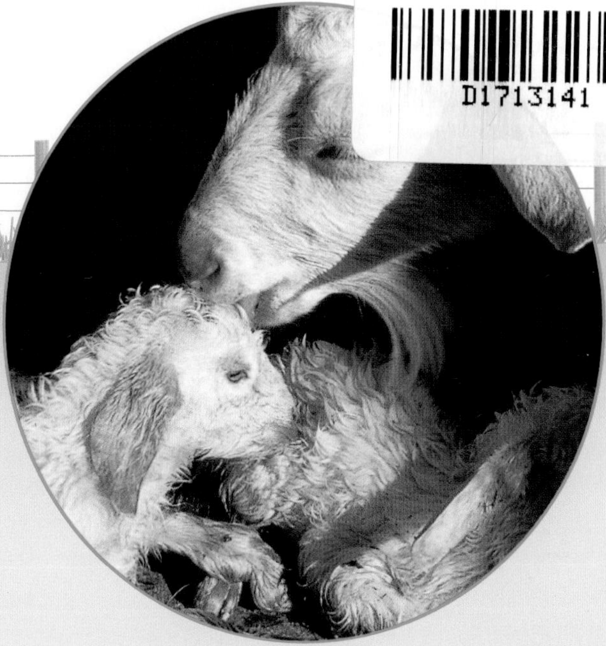

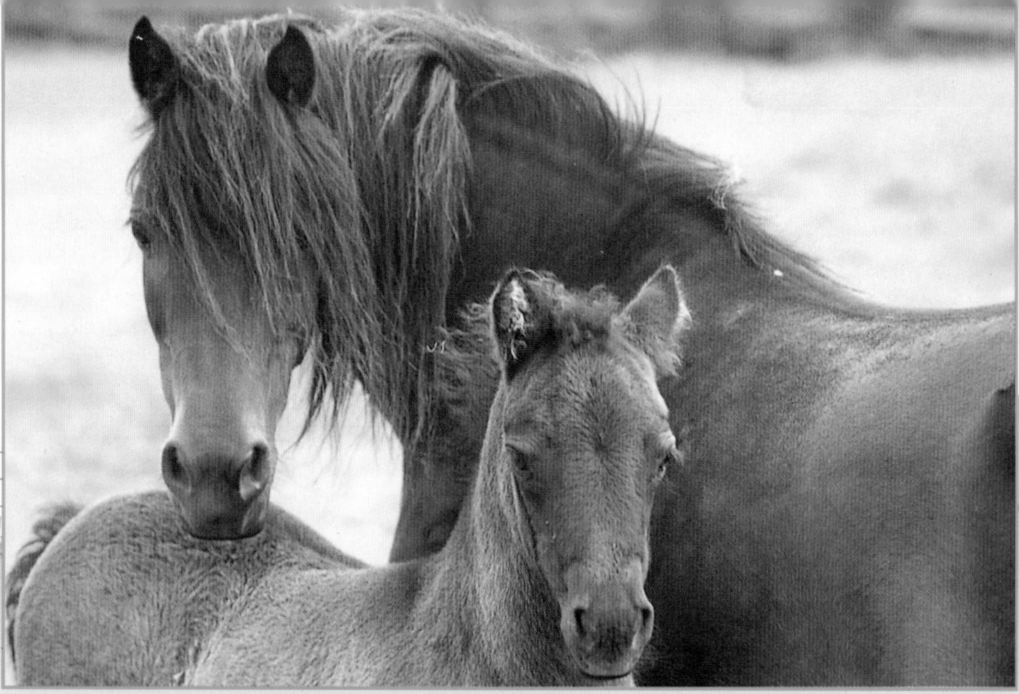

Horses live on a farm.

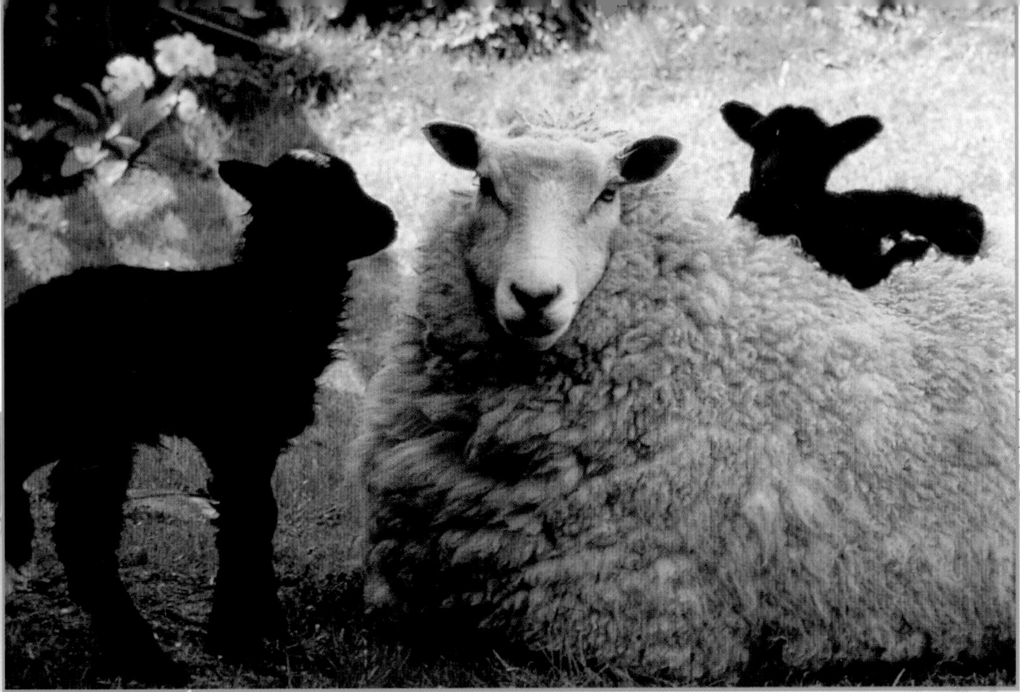

Sheep live on a farm.

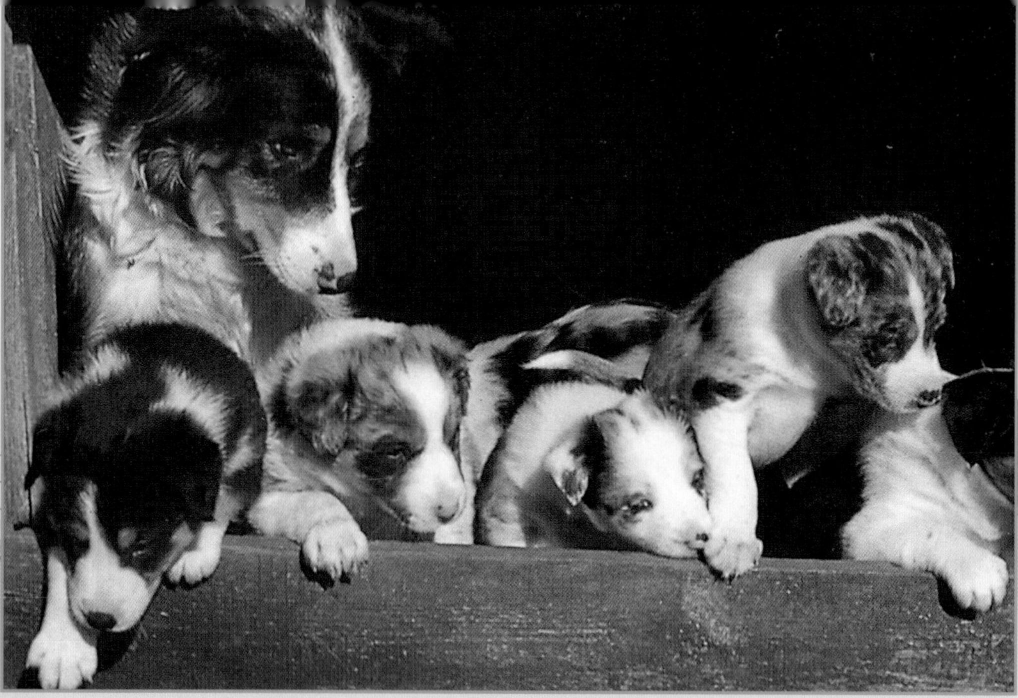

Dogs live on a farm.

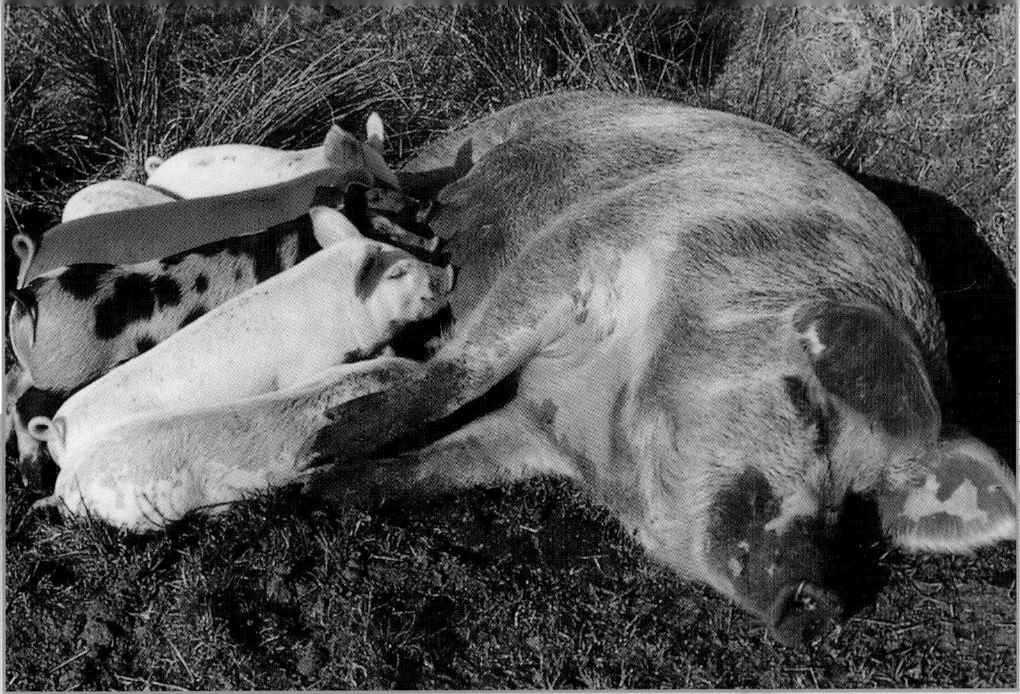

Pigs live on a farm.

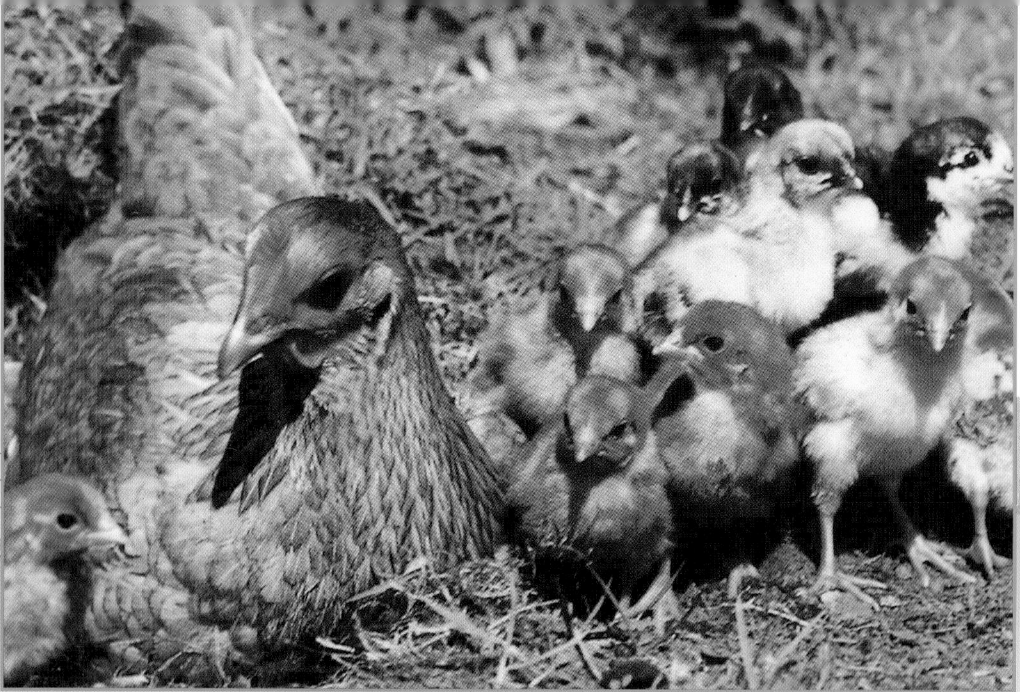

Chickens live on a farm.

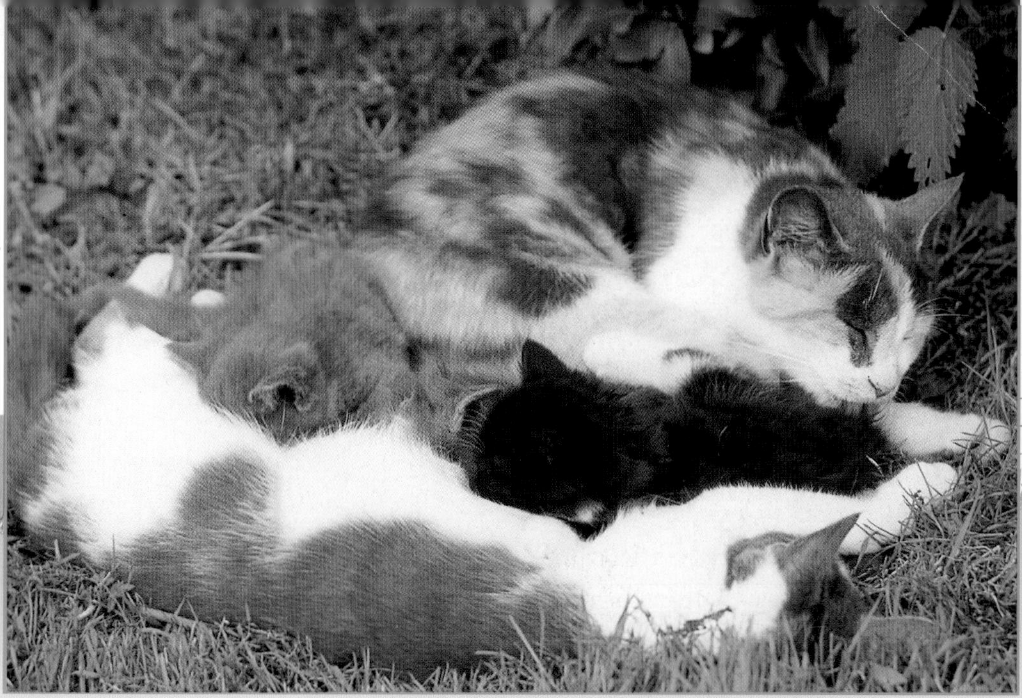

Cats live on a farm.

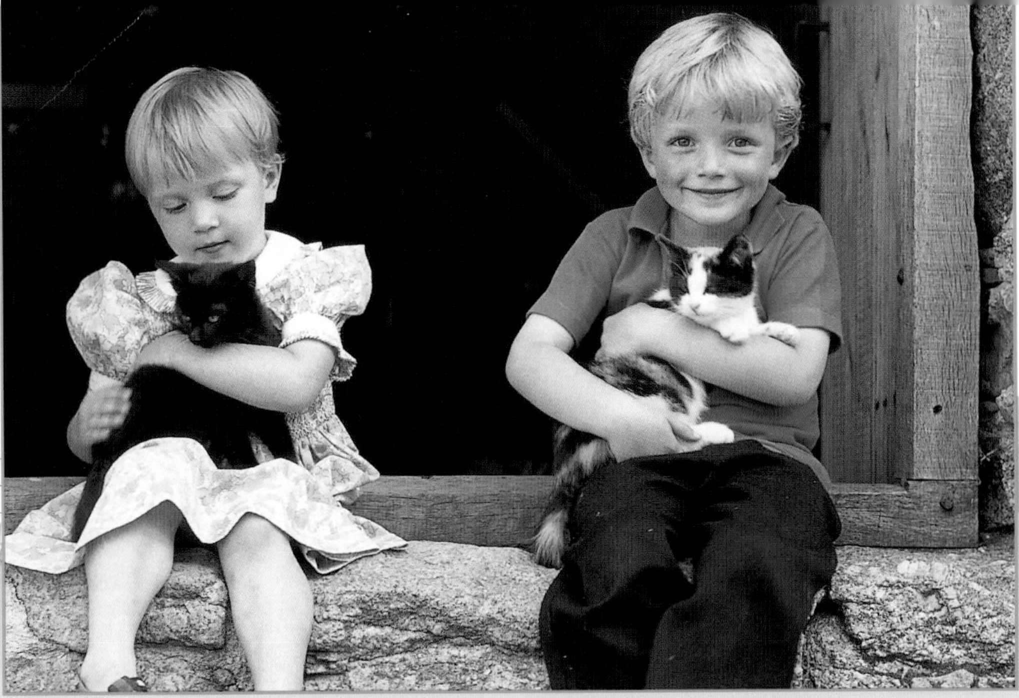

Children live
on a farm, too!